T0201726

Dog Dude

THIS EDITION

Editorial Management by Oriel Square
Produced for DK by WonderLab Group LLC
Jennifer Emmett, Erica Green, Kate Hale, *Founders*

Editor Maya Myers; **Photography Editor** Nicole DiMella; **Managing Editor** Rachel Houghton;
Designers Project Design Company; **Researcher** Michelle Harris;
Copy Editor Lori Merritt; **Indexer** Connie Binder; **Proofreader** Susan K. Hom;
Series Reading Specialist Dr. Jennifer Albro

First American Edition, 2024
Published in the United States by DK Publishing, a division of Penguin Random House LLC
1745 Broadway, 20th Floor, New York, NY 10019

Text and Illustration Copyright © Wonderlab Group, LLC 2024
24 25 26 27 10 9 8 7 6 5 4 3 2 1
001-342891-Oct/2024

A catalog record for this book is available from the Library of Congress.
HC ISBN: 978-0-5938-4725-1
PB ISBN: 978-0-5938-4724-4

DK books are available at special discounts when purchased in bulk for sales promotions, premiums, fund-raising,
or educational use. For details, contact:
DK Publishing Special Markets, 1745 Broadway, 20th Floor, New York, NY 10019
SpecialSales@dk.com

Printed and bound in China

The publisher would like to thank the following for their kind permission to reproduce their images:
a=above; c=center; b=below; l=left; r=right; t=top; b/g=background
Alamy Stock Photo: © Hanna-Barbera / Courtesy Everett Collection 26cla, © Paramount Pictures / Courtesy:
Everett Collection. 27cl, © United Features Syndicate / Courtesy Everett Collection 27tl, © Walt Disney Co. /
Courtesy Everett Collection 27crb, PA Images / Peter Nicholls 26cr, Pictorial Press Ltd 27cra; **Depositphotos Inc:**
Dasha9534 6-7; **Dorling Kindersley:** Wonderlab - Gaz Weisman 11tr, 12cra, 16bc, 27tr; **Dreamstime.com:**
Adogslifephoto 8bl, 9tr, 9bc, Igor Akimov 12tl, Alsimonov 26-27, Vassilis Anastasiou 19tl, Yuri Arcurs 29crb, Ryhor
Bruyeu 23tr, Roman Chazov 25tr, Judith Dzierzawa 8br, 9bl (br), Ecophoto 13tr, Roman Egorov 14cr, Farinoza 8tr,
9ca, Przemyslaw Iciak 14c, Sari Juurinen 20tl, Lightfieldstudiosprod 23tl, Makc76 16br, Irina Meshcheryakova 3,
Mexitographer 29tl, Muro123 13b, Jaroslav Noska 24t, Alejandro Prez 1, Smrm1977 (null) 15b, Tartilastock 7t, 20bl,
24crb, 26br, 30, Karoline Thalhofer 18, Madelein Wolfaardt 20br; **Getty Images:** Eugene Gologursky / Stringer
26bl, Mint Images RF 22b, Andrew Toth / Stringer 26cra; **Getty Images / iStock:** E+ / Andyworks 10, E+ /
elenaleonova 4-5, E+ / GeorgePeters 28b, E+ / RichLegg 25bl, Fenne 16bl, Maike Hildebrandt 11cla (album),
MINIWIDE 11cla, Evgeniya_Mokeeva 4-5 (HeadbandX3), 6cb (x2), 8cb (propsx2), 9cb (propsx2), 24crb (hat), 28cb
(propsx4), SVPhilon 12tr, vojce 17, Aleksandr Zotov 19br; **Shutterstock.com:** cfg1978 27bl, Jucadima 29tr, Stayer
22cr, Tawnya92 21**Nicole DiMella/WonderLab Group:** 9cra

Cover images: *Front:* **Shutterstock.com:** Javier Brosch; *Back:* **Shutterstock.com:** Rita_Kochmarjova cra

All other images © Dorling Kindersley Limited
For more information see: www.dkimages.com

www.dk.com

MIX
Paper | Supporting
responsible forestry
FSC™ C018179

This book was made with Forest
Stewardship Council™ certified
paper – one small step in DK's
commitment to a sustainable future.
Learn more at
www.dk.com/uk/information/sustainability

Dog Dude

Becky Baines

Contents

What's Up, Dogs?

Wrinkly noses and soft, furry ears. Wagging tails and wiggly cuddles. Sweet puppy paws and warm puppy breath. Dogs are cool dudes!

Howl you doin'?

Dogs are one of the most diverse animal species on the planet. The smallest dogs are only about the size of a hedgehog. The biggest can weigh as much as a lion. They can be fluffy or smooth. They can be roly-poly or strong—or both!

How can our furry friends be so different from each other? Humans helped them get that way!

Mom

Dad

Mutt Matters

There are between 200 and 400 dog breeds. It's hard to agree on the number. This is because what makes a breed can be a little fuzzy. If two dogs of different breeds have a puppy, they make a whole new kind of dog. Dogs that are a mix of a bunch of breeds are called mutts!

Let's Get Wild

A long time ago, wolves were the only canines around. They lived in the forest in packs. They stayed far away from humans.

Oooooo ooooooooww wwwwww! Get off my paw!

This changed when people started living in villages. The humans left bones and scraps of food on the ground. Wolves began to sniff around. They ate the leftovers.

Humans liked the free trash removal. Wolves liked the free meals. A great friendship was born!

Is being handsome a job?

Humans learned they could train dogs to do jobs. They also found out they could help make dogs with super skills! They matched up different types of dogs to have puppies with the traits of both parents. This is called breeding.

Born to Be Not-So-Wild

Other animals have been bred by humans, too. Pigs, goats, horses, and cats were all wild once!

As pups were bred for certain jobs, their looks began to change. Rat catchers had short legs for digging holes. Hunting dogs had long snouts for sniffing. Dogs bred for pulling had strong shoulders.

What would your perfect dog be able to do?

Super Senses

Dogs may look different, but they all have something in common. All dogs have paw-some senses!

I swear it's not me.

Smell

Dogs have up to 300 million smell receptors in their noses. Humans have only six million. And compared to humans, dogs use 40 percent more of their brain just for smelling. Talk about a superpower!

Hearing

Dogs also have super hearing. Your dog may bark at a sound well before you hear it. Or maybe you won't hear it at all!

A dog whistle makes a sound so high that humans can't hear it. But dogs can! Dogs can hear noises at pitches three times higher than humans can hear! The pitch is how high or low a sound is.

Taste

Dogs don't have as many taste buds as people do. But they do have special taste buds for tasting water. They also have taste buds in the back of their throats. So, when they are gulping down food, they probably still taste it!

Slurp!

Mmmm... Bone appetit!

Sight

Dogs see a blurry world in mostly blue, yellow, and gray. But they can see very well at night. Their field of vision is much bigger, too. That means they see things in motion more clearly. Watch out, squirrels!

Naughty by Nature?

Why does my dog...

...drink out of the toilet?
Some dogs like toilet water because it's colder than the stuff in their bowls. It's also fresher from all the flushing.

Refreshing!

...pee on trees? Dogs pee on grass, trees, and fire hydrants to tell other dogs, "Hey, this is my turf!" Dogs will also pee on spots where other dogs have gone before them.

...sniff butts? Think of this as a doggy handshake. Each dog has its own scent. The scent is strongest near its rear. When your dog sniffs another dog's rump, they're getting to know a friend.

...roll in stinky stuff?

Wolves try to hide their own scent so they can sneak up on their next meal. Even though pet dogs don't need to hunt for food, the habit stuck around.

...bury bones? Hiding food is also a habit from the wild. Dogs protect leftovers so they won't run out of food. Your dog is saving its bone for a rainy day.

Where did it go?

...give "kisses" with licks?

In their pack, wolves groom each other with their tongues. Dogs do the same. When your dog licks you, they're saying, "I love you."

Mwah!

Built-In Besties

In the wild, each wolf has a job to do to take care of its pack. Without a pack to run around with, dogs make you their pack!

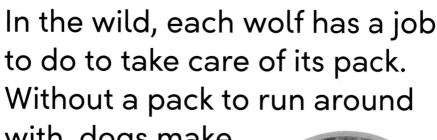

Dogs' built-in need to please people makes it easy to teach them tricks and skills that can be funny, cute, or helpful. Training dogs to follow commands like SIT, STAY, COME, and OFF is good for helping dogs learn to be polite. Dogs can be trained to do very important jobs, too!

Doggy detective on the case.

Search and Rescue

If a person is missing, search-and-rescue dogs might be sent in to find them. Dogs can smell through water or snow.
They can smell under rocks and rubble.

Support Dogs

Dogs are so tuned in to the needs of humans that they can be very helpful for people with disabilities. Emotional support dogs can provide extra comfort and care to help people do things they have trouble with on their own.

Sniffer Dogs

Dogs can be trained to sniff out any sort of scent. They can smell for explosives or fruit. This helps to keep people safe.

Famous Furry Friends

Scooby-Doo

Boo

Queen Elizabeth II's corgis

Bluey

No paw-parazzi, please.

To the Rescue!

There are close to a billion dogs in the world. Many millions of them need homes. To find the perfect pup for you, dog rescues and shelters are a good place to look.

At a shelter, you can find dogs of all different ages, breeds, shapes, and sizes. All they need is a chance to find their forever home.

Not-So-Bad to the Bone

Dogs that have to protect themselves in the wild develop defenses. If a street dog has had bad experiences, it may growl or show its teeth. But with training and love, most pups can become good pets!

Glossary

Breed
A type of dog with similar appearance, size, and behavior

Breeding
To match up dogs so their puppies will have certain traits

Canine
The family of animals that includes dogs, wolves, coyotes, foxes, and jackals

Command
A way of telling a dog to do something

Defenses
Natural behavior to avoid being harmed by another

Diverse
Having a lot of different traits or varieties within a group

Groom
To care for and clean

Pack
A group of animals, like wolves

Receptor
A cell that receives information and sends it to the brain

Species
A group of living things that shares characteristics and is able to reproduce

Train
To teach to do something a certain way

Trait
Something special about the way a living thing looks or behaves

Index

Quiz

Answer the questions to see what you have learned. Check your answers in the key below.

1. Why did wolves first start to sniff around human villages?

2. What is it called when humans match two dogs up to make puppies that have certain traits?

3. What is a dog's ultimate super sense?

4. How can you get a dog to follow commands?

5. True or False: Dogs can smell through water and snow.

1. Looking for leftover bones and scraps 2. Breeding 3. Smell
4. Training 5. True